The Garden Invention Invasion

Written by Becca Heddle

Illustrated by Marina Pérez Luque

Collins

Lucy and Reece live in a town. The house next to theirs has a lovely garden, full of picturesque plants.

The house belongs to Mrs Knox. But no one ever sees her in the garden. It's a mystery.

"Mrs Knox is probably a magician," says Reece.

"She might just be shy," says Lucy.

One hot night, Lucy and Reece are restless. "I'm sure I heard a noise," says Reece.

Lucy quietly creeps to the window and stares in amazement.

Mrs Knox's garden is full of contraptions. One measures hedges and cuts them into perfect circles.

A second invention snips scented flowers and places them by the door.

"Reece!" whispers Lucy. "Come quickly!"

He looks out into the darkness too, and watches the mechanical gadgets with excitement.

"How clever!" he says softly.

"Now we know for sure that Mrs Knox isn't a magician," says Reece. "She's an engineer."

But they don't notice the mice in Mrs Knox's garden.
And one night, the mice wriggle into her shed, to make
themselves a place to sleep.

The mice settle in happily and make a nest.
Their fearless babies gnaw on the wires and knobs
that work the contraptions.

Late one moonless night, Mrs Knox is sleeping heavily when something goes "pop". An invention stops trimming the hedge and zooms off, wrecking the fence.

"Pop!" "Zap!" "Zop!" There are several small explosions. Now all the contraptions are malfunctioning. They head merrily down the road.

In the morning, there is a scene of devastation. The gadgets are still in motion, slicing into borders and snipping plants into circles and squares.

"This is disgraceful!" cries a neighbour, angrily. "These vicious contraptions have turned our town into a crazy circus!"

Reece and Lucy race to Mrs Knox's house and knock on the door.

"Yes?" she asks, worriedly, as she opens it.

Lucy explains, breathlessly, "Your inventions are wrecking the town!"

Mrs Knox gasps. "How dreadful!" she says. "I'll get some emergency tools."

She grabs some wrenches, a tennis racquet and squashy balls.

Mrs Knox's feet are a blur of motion as she runs.
She bounces balls at her inventions with the tennis racquet,
to jam the wheels.

Now the contraptions have stopped, she uses her wrench to turn off knobs. She works tirelessly until every gadget is lying in pieces in the street.

Reece whoops in triumph. But Mrs Knox is tearful.

"I'm so sorry," she says. "I don't know why my inventions went wrong."

Then a neighbour notices the mice. "These might have something to do with it," he says gently. "They need a proper home!"

The neighbour helps Mrs Knox mend her fence. Lucy and Reece make an exhibition of photos showing the inventions and the mess they had made of the gardens.

Now Mrs Knox knows her neighbours, she starts teaching them about engineering. Her inventions help to tidy up the mess.

Best Kept Gardens

Mechanical mayhem

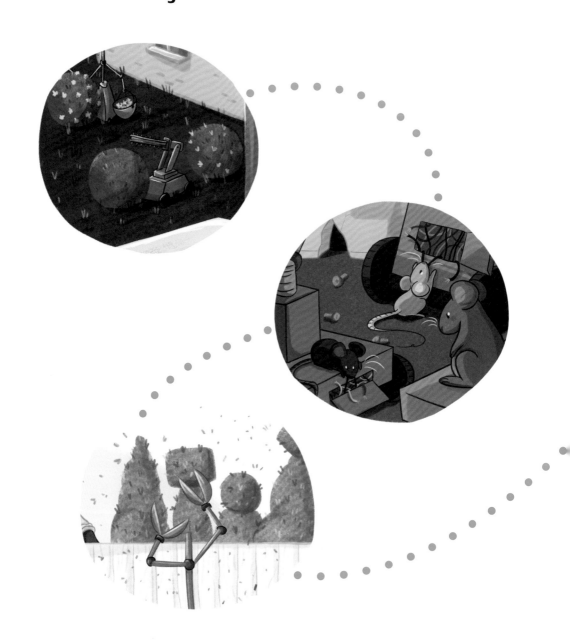

After reading

Letters and Sounds: Phases 5–6

Word count: 483

Focus phonemes: /n/ kn, gn /r/ wr /s/ c, ce, sc /c/ qu /zh/ s, si /sh/ ti, ci, s

Common exception words: of, to, the, into, are, do, one, our, their, Mrs, says, door

Curriculum links: Design and technology

National Curriculum learning objectives: Reading/word reading: apply phonic knowledge and skills as the route to decode words, read common exception words, noting unusual correspondences between spelling and sound and where these occur in the word; read other words of more than one syllable that contain taught GPCs; Reading/comprehension: develop pleasure in reading, motivation to read, vocabulary and understanding by being encouraged to link what they read or hear to their own experiences

Developing fluency

- Your child may enjoy hearing you read the book.
- Take turns to read two to four pages of text, encouraging different voices for the characters, and varying tone and emphasis.

Phonic practice

- Challenge your child to read these words. What different spellings can they find that make the /sh/ sound? (*s, ti, ci*)

  exhibition   magician   motion   sure   devastation   vicious

- Ask your child to read these words and find the words that contain the /zh/ sound. (*measures, invasion*)

  picturesque   invasion   measures   wrecking

Extending vocabulary

- Challenge your child to make new words by adding -ness, -less, -tion, -ing or -ly to the following.

  kind (*kindness, kindly*)   invent (*invention, inventing*)   sleep (*sleepless, sleeping*)

- Can your child think of a sentence using each of their new words?